来到中国

STEP INTO
CHINA

Text and Photographs by
NEIL JOHNSON

Julian Messner ⓦ New York
A Division of Simon & Schuster, Inc.

Acknowledgment:
The author would like to thank the
Centenary College Choir for their
inspiration and assistance in
making this book possible.

To Marcus

Calligraphy by Loretta Pan

Copyright © 1988 by Neil Johnson. All rights reserved including the right of reproduction in whole or in part in any form. Published by Julian Messner, a Division of Simon & Schuster, Inc. Simon & Schuster Building, Rockefeller Center, 1230 Avenue of the Americas, New York, NY 10020. JULIAN MESSNER and colophon are trademarks of Simon & Schuster, Inc. Designed by G. Laurens.

Manufactured in the United States of America.

10 9 8 7 6 5 4 3 2 1-Lib. ed. 10 9 8 7 6 5 4 3 2 1-Pbk. ed.

Library of Congress Cataloging in Publication Data

Johnson, Neil. Step into China. Summary: Text and photographs depict contemporary daily life in China. 1. China—Social life and customs—1976— —Juvenile literature. [1. China—Social life and customs] I. Title. DS779.23.J63 1988 951.05'8 87-20274

ISBN 0-671-64338-X-Lib. ed.   ISBN 0-671-65852-2-Pbk. ed.

Many years ago, a wise Chinese man said, "A journey of a thousand miles must begin with a single step."

I hope this book will be the first step on your way to learning about China.

CHINA

China is a country with a history going back thousands of years. Paper, silk, and rockets were all invented in China long ago.

China is one of the world's biggest countries, with high mountains and barren deserts, so most of its people live along the east coast near the ocean and rivers. It has been a Communist country for less than forty years.

Today, one billion people, one out of every five people on earth, live in China under crowded conditions.

What do they do each day?

早上

MORNING

Meiling wakes up in the morning on this school day and puts on a red, yellow, and blue skirt. Not too long ago, people in China wore only dark blue or dark green, but now bright-colored clothes are everywhere.

After she eats some steamed bread and an egg for breakfast, Meiling walks to school through the park near her house. She likes to listen to the songbirds in their cages.

The old men of China raise pet birds for their songs. Each morning, they take them to the park and enjoy their singing, while they talk to their friends in the cool morning air.

学校

SCHOOL

China is not as modern a country as the Chinese want it to be, so education and schools are very important.

In class, Chen listens closely to the teacher to learn as much as possible. He and the other students study how to read and write. He learns why October 1 is a celebration day every year. That was the day in 1949 the People's Republic of China was founded, the day the Communists won the revolution.

For Chinese children, school lasts most of the day, six days a week. Parents sometimes hire a tutor for children so they can continue their lessons.

饭和茶

RICE AND TEA

Luo, like most other southern Chinese, eats rice every day. He is a farmer who plants rice by hand in flooded fields called paddies. Rice needs a large amount of water in order to grow. The rice you eat may be white, but the plant is a rich green when growing.

Tea is the most popular drink in China because it makes food taste better and is believed to make a person healthy. Tea leaves are picked from the plants by hand.

香蕉和船

BANANAS AND BOATS

Ling works on a farm growing bananas. When the bananas begin to ripen, he loads them onto his small boat and floats down the river to the nearby city.

When he gets there, many other farmers are at the landing with their bananas. Food sellers come to the river landing to buy the fruit and then sell it to the people living in the city. Ling sells his bananas to a woman who carries the heavy load away to a street market.

市场 # MARKET

When Lee wants to buy food, he goes to the market. Some markets are along the city streets, where the different foods are laid out for everyone to see and buy. Lee must go to market almost every day because he does not have a refrigerator to keep his food fresh.

Bread, eggs and many types of vegetables are sold at the markets. Fish, live chickens and shrimp laid out in the open fill the street market with many strong smells.

When Lee decides to buy some vegetables, the seller weighs them on a hanging scale to see how much Lee should pay.

游戏

GAMES

The people of China like to laugh and play games. Ping pong, badminton, volleyball, and swimming are popular in China. Cheuk works in Beijing, the capital of China. During his morning break he likes to play soccer with his friends.

Fireworks were invented in China. Today when there is something to celebrate, a string of firecrackers is hung in a tree. Lighted from the bottom, they go off in a long and loud stream of explosions. Everybody covers his or her ears and laughs until it is finally quiet again.

工作 WORK

China is not dependent on machines. Much of the work is done in the same way it has been done for hundreds of years. From carrying loads to planting crops to making goods in factories, the men and women of China get the work done without machines.

Many people work in the fields planting and harvesting. Sometimes they may use tractors to till the soil, but mostly they use strong water buffalo to pull the plows.

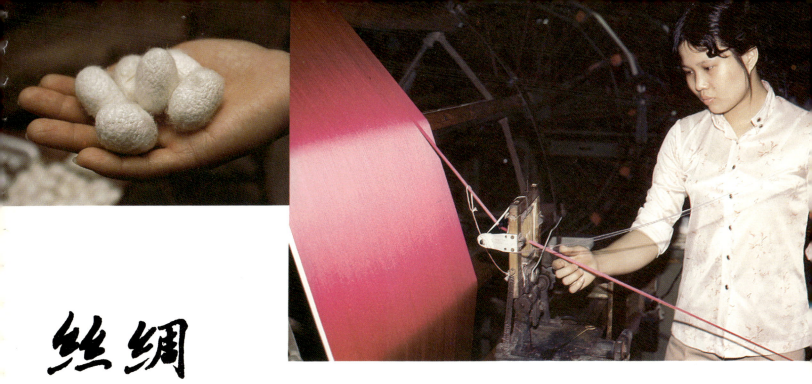

丝绸

SILK

China discovered that the finest cloth in the world, silk, can be produced from the small, white cocoons of silkworms.

Every day in China the fine fibers from cocoons are spun into thread at the silk factory where Su Kwan works. The silk thread is dyed many colors and, by the end of the day, woven into beautiful fabric for clothes.

算盘
ABACUS

To do arithmetic, a simple calculator with sliding wooden beads called an abacus is used. The abacus has not changed in six hundred years.

In the stores of China, there are no cash registers. The salespeople count and do arithmetic on abacuses. Many Chinese children can use an abacus as fast as an electronic calculator.

语言
LANGUAGE

In the Chinese language, there is no alphabet. The Chinese words are called characters. They are like word pictures.

Many Chinese can read and write characters, but it is very difficult and takes many years for a person to learn to write the whole Chinese character language. Those few scholars who can do it are respected artists.

算盘
ABACUS

To do arithmetic, a simple calculator with sliding wooden beads called an abacus is used. The abacus has not changed in six hundred years.

In the stores of China, there are no cash registers. The salespeople count and do arithmetic on abacuses. Many Chinese children can use an abacus as fast as an electronic calculator.

语言
LANGUAGE

In the Chinese language, there is no alphabet. The Chinese words are called characters. They are like word pictures.

Many Chinese can read and write characters, but it is very difficult and takes many years for a person to learn to write the whole Chinese character language. Those few scholars who can do it are respected artists.

丝绸

SILK

China discovered that the finest cloth in the world, silk, can be produced from the small, white cocoons of silkworms.

Every day in China the fine fibers from cocoons are spun into thread at the silk factory where Su Kwan works. The silk thread is dyed many colors and, by the end of the day, woven into beautiful fabric for clothes.

河流
RIVERS

In China, wherever possible, the people still use rivers and canals for transportation, just as they have for centuries. Large Chinese sailboats called junks were quite common before boats began using motors.

Boats of all sizes are used for travel and to carry loads of different goods. Many people even live on their houseboats. The waterways are always very busy with boat traffic because, in many ways, it is the easiest way to travel in China.

自行车

BICYCLES

There are few cars in China. However, every day in the cities the streets are crowded with people on bicycles. Here they are not used as toys or for exercise, but for transportation.

Mostly colored black, the bicycles are parked in parking lots and repaired in roadside stations just as cars are in other countries.

Except when they take very long trips, most people travel on foot or by bicycle. Some people use three-wheeled, heavy-duty tricycles in place of trucks to carry heavy loads.

文化

CULTURE

Tao loves music. When she was five years old, a teacher at her kindergarten interested her in the violin. After two years of study with a violin teacher, she is becoming quite good.

China has a long history of fine art. It is hard to believe, but for a while not too long ago, art was against the law. Today, though, art is again very important to the Chinese people.

Lei-li works in a porcelain factory painting designs on large, elegant vases. It takes long hours of delicate work to finish one vase.

FAMILY

A family living in a Chinese house might include not only the parents and child, but also grandparents and maybe even a few aunts, uncles, and cousins.

Because Chinese cities are so crowded, parents usually have only one child. This one child is loved dearly. The parents try to give the child everything he or she needs, especially the best education possible.

结论

CONCLUSION

Each day in China is much like a day anywhere.

   People eat and sleep, go to school, play soccer and enjoy music, grow roses, and work at factories, farms, businesses, and with their families.

   But in many ways, China is different from other countries. This ancient and complex land is not like any other because it is so old and so big and has such a special history. Some people come from other lands and spend many years of their lives on the fascinating journey to understanding China.